AF264380

Paradise on Earth

Jermaine Donaldson

Disclaimer

This book explores complex moral, political, and social themes, including power, leadership, conflict, and the consequences of extreme decisions. The views, philosophies, and actions expressed within this narrative belong solely to the fictional characters and do not represent the personal beliefs or endorsements of the author.

This work is intended to provoke thought and reflection, not to promote violence, authoritarianism, or harm. The story examines how individuals and societies are shaped by circumstances, emphasizing that people are not born villains, but are often molded by systems, trauma, and moral conflict.

Readers are encouraged to engage critically with the material, reflect on its ethical questions, and form their own conclusions. This book is offered as a work of imagination and inquiry, not instruction or advocacy.

PROLOGUE

The world did not collapse in a single moment. It learned how to live with its own decay. Hunger became statistics, war became policy, and suffering became something people scrolled past rather than confronted. Systems built to protect humanity began protecting power instead, and over time, injustice stopped feeling shocking and started feeling normal.

For generations, leaders promised peace while preserving imbalance. Nations mastered control but abandoned responsibility. Humanity advanced in technology yet stalled in compassion, waiting for change while refusing its cost. The world did not lack solutions, it lacked the will to choose them. Neutrality became easier than courage, and silence proved deadlier than violence.

This is not the story of a hero, but of a man who refused to accept that suffering was inevitable. When dialogue failed and patience protected corruption, he faced a truth the world avoids: paradise is not a dream. it is a decision. And decisions, unlike hopes, demand action.

DEDICATION

This book is not dedicated to one name, one place, or one moment.

It is offered to anyone willing to look at the world honestly.

It is for those who believe in kindness, yet understand that kindness alone does not always stop injustice. For those who know that people are not born villains, but are shaped by the weight of a broken world. For those who wrestle with the uncomfortable truth that doing what is right may sometimes require extreme decisions.

This work is shared as light, not judgment. May it challenge, awaken, and remind us that a better world is possible, not because we are perfect, but because we are responsible.

Contents

CHAPTER 1

WORLD IN CHAOS

The world did not fall apart all at once. It fractured slowly, day by day, headline by headline, scream by scream. Isaac had learned that chaos did not always arrive with explosions. Sometimes it crept in quietly through television screens, whispered through news feeds, and lived in the tired faces of people who no longer believed things would get better.

At thirty-four years old, Isaac had seen more than enough of it. He stood in his apartment in Israel, the television glowing against the dimness of the room. The sound was low, but the images were loud.

Cities burning. Crowds running. Children crying. Soldiers shouting orders in languages Isaac recognized and others he did not. Different countries, different borders, but the suffering looked the same everywhere. War. Corruption. Racism. Poverty. Power held by men who never paid the price for their decisions.

Isaac folded his arms across his chest and exhaled slowly. He had watched scenes like this countless times, yet something about tonight felt heavier. The images refused to blur into background noise. They pressed against his mind, demanding attention.

"How many more?" he muttered to himself.

On the screen, a reporter spoke urgently about another conflict escalating, another peace agreement collapsing before the ink had dried. Isaac reached for the remote and turned the volume up.

"This violence is the result of years of political failure and unchecked authority," the reporter said. *"Civilians continue to suffer while global leaders debate responsibility."*

Isaac shook his head. Debate. Always debate. Endless-meetings, empty speeches, promises made for cameras and forgotten the moment the lights went out.

He turned off the television, but the images stayed with him. Isaac had always been observant. Even as a child, he noticed things other people ignored. The way anger traveled faster than compassion. The way power protected itself. The way suffering became statistics when it lasted too long. He did not see the world in absolutes of good and evil. He saw repetition. And repetition, he believed, was humanity's greatest failure.

Earlier that day, he had walked through a crowded street market, listening more than speaking. Vendors argued over prices. A mother pulled her child close as soldiers passed nearby. An elderly man sat against a wall, eyes empty, hand outstretched. Isaac had stopped and offered him water.

"Thank you," the man said softly, his voice worn thin by years of disappointment.

"What happened to you?" Isaac asked.

The man gave a small, humorless laugh. *"What happens to everyone. The world moves on."*

Those words followed Isaac long after he walked away.

Now, standing alone in his apartment, he replayed them in his mind. The world moves on. It always did. Over graves. Over ruins. Over broken promises.

Isaac sat down at the small table near the window and

stared out at the city lights. Israel was alive tonight. Cars moved. People talked. Life continued. And yet beneath it all was tension, like a fault line waiting to break.

He had grown up believing in dialogue. In patience. In the idea that if people talked long enough, listened carefully enough, they could resolve anything. He believed in compromise, in moral responsibility, in leaders who served rather than ruled.

But belief alone did not stop bullets.

His phone buzzed on the table. A message from a colleague.

"Another emergency meeting tomorrow. Same agenda. Same arguments."

Isaac typed back. *"Any solutions?"*

A pause. Then a reply. *"You already know the answer."*

Isaac placed the phone face down.

He thought of the people he had met during his early political work. Factory workers struggling to feed their families. Refugees who no longer remembered what safety felt like. Students who spoke passionately about justice and quietly wondered if it was pointless.

They were not angry because they hated the world. They were angry because they loved it and felt betrayed. And that was what disturbed Isaac the most. Not just the violence, but the exhaustion. Humanity was tired. Tired of waiting for leaders who never arrived. Tired of systems that protected the powerful and punished the weak.

He leaned back in his chair and closed his eyes.

Why does it always end like this?

The question had no easy answer. It never had.

Earlier that week, Isaac had attended a diplomatic gathering where representatives from multiple nations spoke eloquently about peace. They shook hands. They smiled. They posed for photographs.

Later, in private rooms away from cameras, the conversations changed.

"We cannot risk losing control," one leader had said.

"Our economy would collapse if we agreed to that," another had replied.

"What about the people?" Isaac had asked.

The room had gone quiet.

Someone cleared their throat. *"We must be realistic."*

Realistic. Isaac had learned that word often meant indifferent.

Now, alone with his thoughts, he replayed that moment. The silence. The way eyes had avoided his. The unspoken agreement that suffering was acceptable as long as power remained intact.

He stood up and paced the room, frustration tightening his chest. He was not naive. He knew the world was complicated. He knew there were no perfect solutions. But he also knew that inaction was a choice.

And too many people were choosing it.

Outside, sirens echoed faintly in the distance. Isaac paused near the window and watched as a group of young men argued loudly on the street below. Their voices rose, fueled by anger and fear. A passerby hurried away.

This is how it starts, Isaac thought. Not with leaders, but with people pushed too far.

He remembered a conversation from years earlier, one that had stayed with him.

"You really think humanity can change?" a friend had asked him.

"Yes," Isaac had replied without hesitation.

"How?"

"By refusing to accept what is broken as normal."

That belief still lived inside him, stubborn and unyielding. Despite everything he had seen, he refused to believe that violence was humanity's destiny. He refused to believe that racism, poverty, and corruption were permanent features of existence rather than failures of will.

He sat back down and opened his notebook, flipping through pages filled with observations, questions, fragments of ideas. He had been writing for years, not plans exactly, but thoughts. These had been reflections on systems that failed and why they failed.

Education mattered. Equality mattered. Accountability mattered. But none of it worked without courage.

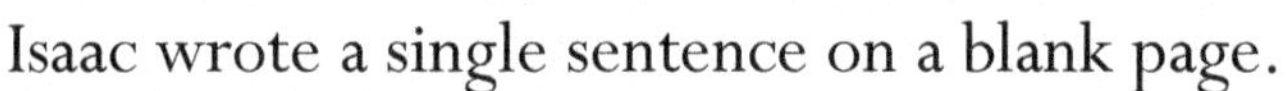

Isaac wrote a single sentence on a blank page.

Humanity can do better.

He stared at the words for a long moment. They felt fragile. Hope often did. But they were honest.

His phone buzzed again. This time, it was his sister.

"Are you watching the news?" she asked when he answered.

"I was sometime back. What happened?"

"It feels like it's getting worse."

Isaac hesitated. *"It feels like we are seeing it more clearly."*

She sighed. *"What can one person do?"*

He had no polished answer. Only the truth. *"More than we think. Or nothing at all."*

There was silence on the line. Then she said quietly, *"Just be careful."*

"I will," Isaac replied, though he was not entirely sure what that meant.

After the call ended, Isaac remained seated, hands resting on the table. He thought about the responsibility that came with awareness. Once you truly saw the world, you could not unsee it. Once you recognized injustice, neutrality became impossible.

He did not want power. He did not crave control. Authority had always made him uncomfortable. But responsibility was something else entirely.

The suffering of ordinary people weighed on him like a constant pressure. It was there when he woke up and when he tried to sleep. It followed him through meetings, conversations, and quiet moments alike.

Why should children be born into war zones?

Why should skin color determine opportunity?

Why should food be wasted in one country while another starved?

These were not abstract questions to Isaac. They were moral failures masquerading as inevitability.

He stood once more and walked to the window. The city stretched before him, imperfect and alive. Somewhere beyond it, across borders and oceans, millions of others stood in their own cities, asking the same questions in different languages.

Isaac rested his forehead against the glass.

"We can do better," he said aloud, testing the words.

The room did not answer, but something inside him shifted.

He realized then that waiting for change was no longer an option. The world had proven that it would not heal itself. Systems built on exploitation did not suddenly become just. Leaders who benefited from imbalance did not voluntarily dismantle it.

Change required disruption. Not violence, but resolve.

He did not yet know what that change would look like. He did not have a plan. Only a conviction growing stronger by the moment.

Neutrality, he understood, was a luxury afforded to those untouched by suffering.

Isaac was touched by it every day.

As the night deepened, he turned off the lights and

stood in the darkness, listening to the distant sounds of the city. He felt fear, yes. Anyone who claimed otherwise was lying. But fear no longer outweighed responsibility.

The world was broken.

And for the first time, Isaac accepted a truth that would alter everything.

It would not fix itself.

Change would not come through waiting, hoping, or asking politely.

Someone would have to act.

And as the thought settled in his chest, quiet but firm, Isaac knew that someone might have to be him.

CHAPTER 2

MAN BEFORE POWER

Before power ever touched Isaac's hands, he belonged to people.

He grew up in a place that once felt like home, even though outsiders would never have called it safe. As a child, the streets were alive with familiar faces. Neighbors greeted each other by name. Children ran freely between buildings. Doors stayed open longer than they should have, and trust still existed, fragile but real.

Isaac remembered those early years clearly. The laughter, the shared meals and the belief that everyone was watching out for one another.

"It did not always start bad," his mother once told him.

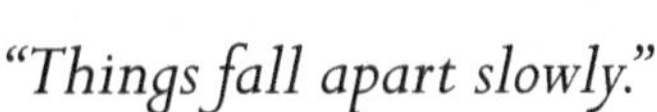

She was right.

War did not arrive with warning sirens at first. It arrived in whispers. In arguments, in tension that settled into the air and refused to leave. Isaac was still young when he noticed people changing. Friends stopped lingering outside. Parents spoke in lower voices. The warmth of the neighborhood cooled into suspicion.

And then violence followed.

By the time Isaac reached his teenage years, the place that once felt like family had become unpredictable and dangerous. People were getting hurt. Some disappeared while others hardened. Survival replaced kindness as the primary concern.

Through it all, his mother remained his anchor. She raised him with firmness and compassion, teaching him that morality mattered even when the world suggested otherwise. They talked often, sometimes late into the night, about right and wrong, about responsibility, about the value of human life.

"Never forget," she told him once as they sat at the small kitchen table, *"every person matters. Even when the world tries*

to convince you they do not."

Isaac believed her.

He wanted to believe that understanding could outpace hatred. That patience could soften even the most rigid hearts. He believed dialogue was not weakness but strength.

As he grew older, he carried those beliefs with him into every interaction.

When neighbors argued, Isaac tried to mediate. When tensions rose, he spoke calmly, urging restraint. When others chose silence, he asked questions.

"You think talking will fix this?" a friend once asked him, frustration sharp in his voice.

"It has to," Isaac replied. *"What is the alternative?"*

At that stage of his life, he could not imagine one. His kindness was not performative. It was instinctive. When he saw hungry families, especially children, he offered what little he had. More than once, he gave away his own meal, ignoring the ache in his stomach.

"You need this more than I do," he told a woman holding a

crying child.

She looked at him in disbelief. *"Why would you do this?"*

Isaac shrugged. *"Because I can."*

He believed community was built through sacrifice, not speeches. Yet again and again, his efforts met resistance. People were tired. They were scared and protective of the little they had left.

"We cannot afford to care about everyone," someone told him.

Isaac disagreed, quietly but firmly.

He tried organizing neighbors, encouraging cooperation, suggesting small changes that could make life easier. Clean shared spaces. Shared resources. Shared responsibility.

Most people refused.

"Worry about yourself," they said. *"That is how you survive."*

Each rejection chipped away at his optimism, though it did not break it.

Despite witnessing growing cruelty, Isaac still believed the world could be repaired without force. He believed reason could reach people if given enough time. That systems failed because people stopped talking to one another.

He was not drawn to authority. Titles made him uncomfortable. Control unsettled him. He preferred persuasion over command, conversation over enforcement. Leadership, to him, was service.

"I do not want power," he told his mother once. *"I just want things to make sense."*

She studied him for a moment. *"Be careful,"* she said. *"The world punishes people who want that."*

Isaac did not fully understand what she meant then.

As war intensified, he began encountering people who treated human life as disposable. Not out of desperation, but out of indifference. Men who spoke of violence casually. Leaders who spoke of loss as numbers rather than names.

These encounters disturbed him deeply.

"How can you talk like that?" Isaac asked one night after

overhearing a conversation about civilian casualties.

The man laughed. *"It is not personal."*

"That is the problem," Isaac replied.

The gap between his values and the reality around him widened. He felt himself standing at a crossroads between who he was taught to be and who the world seemed to reward.

Still, he resisted the idea that force was necessary.

He entered political discussions reluctantly, hoping they could be platforms for change rather than domination. When others pushed for control, he pushed for compromise. When others demanded obedience, he argued for understanding.

"You are too patient," a colleague told him during a heated discussion.

"Maybe," Isaac replied, *"but patience saves lives."*

At least, he believed it did. Yet patience had its limits.

As he became more involved in civic conversations, Isaac noticed how often authority protected itself rather than the people. Leaders spoke about stability while ignoring suffering. Decisions were delayed endlessly, buried under bureaucracy.

He felt torn. He did not trust power, yet he saw how powerless those without it were.

Late one evening, after a long community meeting that achieved nothing, Isaac walked home with his head down.

"Why do you keep trying?" a man called out to him.

Isaac stopped. *"Because someone has to."*

The man scoffed. *"You think you can change anything?"*

Isaac did not answer right away. He looked around at the crumbling buildings, the tired faces, the quiet despair.

"I think we have to believe we can," he finally said.

That belief was becoming harder to hold. The world kept testing him. Every act of kindness seemed met with cruelty. Every attempt at cooperation met with selfishness. His idealism remained, but cracks were forming beneath it. He started to sense that innocence was not something the world allowed people to keep.

One night, sitting with his mother after hearing about another violent incident nearby, Isaac spoke what he had been avoiding.

"What if talking is not enough?" he asked.

She looked at him carefully. *"That is a dangerous question."*

"I know," he said. *"But I cannot stop thinking about it."*

She reached across the table and took his hand. *"Whatever path you choose, remember who you are."*

That was the moment Isaac realized something important.

The man he was before power mattered.

The kindness. The patience. The belief in humanity.

But the world was pushing him, slowly, relentlessly, toward a different version of himself.

And he did not yet know which version would survive.

Isaac felt a shift approaching. It was not sudden nor was it dramatic. But it was inevitable.

Innocence, he understood now, was not lost in one moment.

It was tested.

And the test was coming

CHAPTER 3

BREAKING POINT

There are moments in life that do not arrive with announcements or clarity. They form quietly, pressing inward over years, until something finally gives. Isaac's breaking point did not begin on a single day; it had been developing slowly, long before he understood what was happening to him.

Even as a child, he had seen what war could do to people, not in stories told afterward, not in speeches meant to explain or justify, but in the raw truth unfolding in front of him. He remembered standing still, unable to move, as fear passed from one face to another like a disease. People he had seen laughing only days before now looked hollow, their eyes emptied of trust. He did not yet have the words to explain it, but something inside him cracked.

At first, Isaac told himself it was temporary. Once the violence ended, humanity would return to itself. He believed that suffering had meaning, that systems existed to prevent things from going too far. Even as bombs fell and sirens screamed, he held onto the idea that someone somewhere was in control.

As the years passed, that belief weakened. The violence did not stop. It returned in different forms, under different justifications, but always with the same result. Innocent people paid the price. Children learned fear before hope. Leaders spoke of necessity while families buried their dead. Each time, Isaac felt a tightening in his chest, a silent question forming in his mind:

How does this keep happening?

For years, he tried to answer that question without anger. He told himself that kindness mattered, that patience mattered, that refusing to join cruelty could make a difference. Corruption, he believed, survived only because people allowed it, and refusing to participate was a form of resistance.

But then came the event that stripped those beliefs bare.

It happened in Israel. By then, Isaac was no longer simply

observing history. He was involved. He was thinking, planning, and questioning things most people feared to name aloud. He was imagining a different world, one in which power could not hide behind tradition and fear.

He was not alone. His best friend stood beside him, not as a follower, but as an equal. He had believed in Isaac's vision, even when it frightened him.

"You are going to get yourself killed," his friend warned one night, sitting across from him.

"I am not trying to destroy anything," Isaac replied. *"I am trying to stop destruction."*

The friend studied his face. *"That is what scares me,"* he said quietly. *"People do not like being exposed."*

At the time, Isaac dismissed the concern. They were doing nothing wrong. Talking, questioning, and planning were not crimes.

However, he was naive.

A world leader learned enough of Isaac's intentions to recognize the danger, to understand that if his ideas spread, systems built on greed and control could be challenged. The response was swift and calculated.

His best friend was murdered.

There had been no warning, no chance to intervene. One moment he was alive, planning, debating the right course of action. The next, he was gone, erased as though his life had been nothing more than a message.

Isaac remembered the phone call, the silence afterward, the small room feeling impossibly tight. His hands shook, yet his mind felt strangely blank.

"This does not make sense," he kept saying to anyone who would listen. But it did make sense to those in power. The death had not been accidental. It was intentional, a clear warning upfront, and a reminder that kindness and restraint were weaknesses in the face of absolute authority.

The emotional collapse began immediately. Grief struck first, heavy and suffocating. He replayed conversations over and over, questioning if he had said too much, dragged his friend into danger, or failed to protect him. The guilt was unbearable.

"I should have protected him," he whispered to the empty room. *"This was my responsibility."*
Rage followed grief, burning hotter than the numbness. Sleep eluded him, and when it came, he dreamed of his

friend's frozen face, a disbelief that mirrored his own feelings of helplessness.

Isaac began to perceive the world differently. Systems he once trusted now seemed hollow. Governments, laws, and institutions that claimed to serve humanity appeared to protect only those who abused power.

He questioned everything. *What good was kindness if it allowed monsters to thrive? What value did patience have when people were dying?* He had believed that refusing violence was a moral victory. Now it felt like surrender.

He remembered an argument he had with himself late one night. A version of him, the very same version that had once believed neutrality was noble, now whispered, *"Killing is not the answer."*

"And doing nothing is?" the other part of him asked. Silence followed, and the truth became undeniable. Kindness had limits. It could inspire, yes, but it could also be exploited. Corrupt leaders understood mercy better than anyone, using it against those who believed in it.

The voice of his mother returned in memory. Long before she had passed away, she had grasped his hand tightly. *"Promise me you will try to make the world better,"* she

had said.

"I will," he had promised. *"Without hurting anyone."*

She had smiled, a sad and knowing smile. At the time, he had believed she meant perseverance. Now he realized she might have meant something more complex.

The loss of his best friend had destroyed what little faith remained in traditional systems. Courts did nothing. Investigations went nowhere. Public statements were carefully worded to conceal the truth. Bureaucracy buried reality.

That was when he understood a terrifying truth: no one was coming to fix this.

Isaac made a final attempt at peace. He reached out to those who claimed to want change, listening to committees, plans, and endless timelines.

"It takes time," one official said. *"We have to be realistic."*

"How much time?" Isaac asked. *"How many more deaths?"*

The man avoided his eyes. *"That is just how the world works."*

That answer clarified everything. The world worked this way because people allowed it to. He saw patterns everywhere, greedy leaders willing to sacrifice millions to protect their power, nations bargaining with weapons capable of erasing cities, men in suits speaking calmly about destruction as if it were abstract. Lives were reduced to statistics.

The internal conflict tore at him relentlessly. Part of him still clung to the idea that killing was always wrong. Another part countered, louder with each passing day.

"If you remove the people causing the harm, how many lives do you save?"

He hated the question, and yet he could not ignore its logic.

Even at night, he spoke to the memory of his friend as though he were still present.

"You would not want this," he said aloud. *"You believed in doing better."*

In his mind, the friend's voice answered: *"I believed in stopping them."*

Tears blurred Isaac's vision. *"There has to be another way."*

"Then why did it not work?" the imagined voice asked.

Isaac had no answer.

Rage, grief, and responsibility collided inside him, forming something unfamiliar. He was no longer a man who believed neutrality was moral. To stand aside was now to choose the side of those in power by default. He thought of the voiceless, of the children learning fear before hope, of his friend silenced for daring to believe the world could change.

The decision became inevitable. He would no longer stand in the middle. Neutrality was not peace. It was permission.

"I cannot do nothing anymore," he said to himself, voice steady despite months of turmoil.

The path ahead terrified him. Once crossed, there could be no return. He would be judged, hunted, misunderstood. History would not be kind.

But history had never been kind to the dead either. He understood one final truth:

The world would not change itself.

He was done waiting.

CHAPTER 4

RISING LEADER

Isaac did not step into leadership with ceremony orpermission. There was no official transfer of power, no unanimous vote, no peaceful announcement broadcast to reassure the public. His rise happened in the space where systems failed and people grew desperate enough to follow someone who spoke with clarity instead of caution.

The nation was small, worn down by years of conflict, corruption, and leadership that protected itself before protecting its people. Trust in institutions had eroded slowly, then all at once. By the time Isaac emerged as a figure people listened to, the old structures were already hollow.

He had not planned to lead. Leadership had once made

him uncomfortable, even uneasy. But after everything he had witnessed and lost, standing aside no longer felt like an option. When he spoke, he did not promise miracles. He spoke about order. About responsibility. About rebuilding something functional out of what remained.

At first, it was only conversations. Quiet meetings with community figures, workers, teachers, and former officials who had been pushed aside for refusing to play along with corruption. Isaac listened more than he spoke.

"What do you need?" he asked again and again.

"Safety," one man said.

"Food that lasts," said another.

"Someone who doesn't lie to us," a woman added quietly.

Isaac took notes. He asked questions. He did not offer comfort where none existed. Instead, he spoke plainly.

"This will not be easy," he told them. *"But it can be structured. And structure can bring stability."*

Word spread quickly. People were tired of speeches filled with excuses. Isaac did not speak like a politician trained to avoid responsibility. He spoke like someone who understood consequence.

As unrest grew and the existing leadership faltered, Isaac's influence expanded beyond informal gatherings. Groups began organizing around his ideas. Volunteers stepped forward. Former military officers who had grown disillusioned with the government approached him privately.

"You know this puts a target on you," one of them warned during a late-night meeting.

"I know," Isaac replied. *"But it already exists."*

The turning point came not with a single act of violence, but with refusal. The government issued orders that could not be enforced. Workers did not comply. Security forces hesitated. Loyalty fractured. In the vacuum that followed, Isaac stepped forward, not as a conqueror, but as someone willing to take responsibility when others would not.

His rise was not legal. It was not approved. It was not clean. But it was accepted.

The first weeks of leadership were relentless. Isaac understood that authority without order would collapse immediately. He moved quickly, not with cruelty, but with firmness. Corrupt officials were removed. Supply chains were audited. Emergency councils were formed with people chosen for competence rather than loyalty.

"We do not have time for ego," Isaac said during his first address to the council. *"We either work, or we fail."*

Discipline became the foundation. Curfews were enforced not to control, but to protect. Resources were rationed transparently. For the first time in years, people knew where aid was going and why.

However, some people resisted.

"You're moving too fast," a former official argued during a heated discussion. *"You can't rebuild a nation overnight."*

Isaac met his gaze. *"We are not rebuilding overnight. We are stopping the bleeding."*

Reform followed structure. Schools reopened under new oversight. Community programs replaced patronage networks. Local leaders were held accountable publicly, not behind closed doors. Every decision was documented. The changes were immediate. Crime decreased. Markets stabilized. People began to feel something relief; a feeling that was not familiar.

Public support grew not from propaganda, but from results. When food arrived where it was promised, people noticed. When power stayed on through the night, they noticed. When officials were removed for corruption instead of promoted, they noticed.

Crowds gathered when Isaac spoke, not out of obligation, but curiosity.

"He is the first one who does what he says," someone whispered during one address.

"And he remembers names," another replied.

International attention followed soon after. News outlets questioned how a nation long considered unstable was suddenly functioning with efficiency. Foreign diplomats requested meetings. Analysts debated whether Isaac was a reformer or a threat.

In private, Isaac remained cautious. He understood how quickly perception could shift.

"They will not tolerate this for long," one advisor warned him. "You are exposing way too much."

"Good," Isaac replied. *"Sunlight does that."*

Behind closed doors, he began drafting something larger than immediate reform. He worked late into the night, filling notebooks with ideas that extended far beyond national borders. He mapped patterns of corruption that repeated across nations. He studied how power consolidated itself globally, how resources were hoarded, how suffering was normalized.

The problems were not unique to his country. They were systemic.

One evening, a trusted aide noticed the maps spread across Isaac's desk.

"This isn't just about us anymore, is it?" he asked.

Isaac did not look up. *"It never was."*

He began outlining long-term frameworks. Shared resources. Education reform that emphasized shared humanity over nationalism. Systems that reduced the incentive for greed rather than punished it after the damage was done.

"These are global problems," he said during a private meeting.

"They require global solutions."

The idea was not spoken publicly yet. But it existed. And it was quietly taking shape.

International leaders grew uneasy. Invitations came with conditions. Praise was followed by warnings disguised as concern.

"Stability is good," one diplomat said carefully. *"But radical reform can be destabilizing."*

Isaac smiled politely. *"So can corruption."*

As success continued, the people's faith deepened. They spoke of him as a necessary force, not a savior. Isaac corrected them when he could.

"Do not follow me," he told a gathering once. *"Follow the work."*

Still, he felt the weight of expectation growing heavier Every improvement raised the question of why this could not happen elsewhere. Every solved problem revealed ten more beyond his borders.

Late one night, standing alone on a balcony overlooking the city, Isaac allowed himself a moment of honesty.

"This isn't enough," he said softly.

The city below was quieter than it had been in years. Lights glowed steadily. People slept without fear. It was proof that order could be restored. That suffering was not inevitable.

But it was also a reminder. This peace existed only here. For now.

The thought settled into him, slow and deliberate.

If this could work in one nation, why not others.

The ambition did not announce itself. It did not roar. It whispered.

And Isaac listened.

As dawn approached, he returned to his desk and opened a new notebook. On the first page, he wrote a single sentence.

This cannot stop here.

The leader had risen and something much larger was beginning.

CHAPTER 5

VISION CALLED PARADISE

The idea did not arrive in a moment of triumph. It formed quietly, after the noise of war had settled and the damage was fully visible. Isaac had seen victory before. He had also seen its cost. When the conflict in Israel ended and the land returned to a fragile calm, he did not celebrate the way others expected him to. Instead, he walked through streets where buildings still bore scars and families carried grief that victory speeches could not erase.

What stayed with him was not power, but consequence. He had believed for a long time that systems failed people, not because humans were incapable of goodness, but because leadership was too often rooted in profit, fear, and division. The war forced him to confront that belief in its rawest form. Peace had been restored, yet suffering remained. The contradiction unsettled him.

That was where the question first took shape.

If order could be enforced, why could justice not be designed?

If nations could mobilize for destruction, why could they not mobilize for care?

The idea of Paradise on Earth did not emerge as fantasy or religion. It formed as a moral conclusion. Isaac did not imagine heaven descending from the sky. He imagined a world structured so that cruelty had no incentive and dignity was not rare.

Paradise, to him, meant something precise.

A world without hunger because food was treated as a responsibility, not a commodity. A world without poverty because resources were shared, not hoarded. A world without racism because identity no longer determined survival. A world without crime because desperation no longer ruled behavior.

He said it simply to those closest to him at first.

"Paradise is not perfection," Isaac explained one evening. *"It is balance. It is a world where people no longer have to fight*

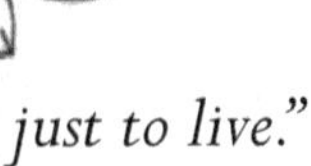

just to live."

One advisor frowned. *"People will say that is impossible."*

Isaac nodded. *"They always do. That does not make it untrue."*

He began to outline the vision as a system rather than a dream. Paradise on Earth was not one nation ruling others. It was a unified global framework rooted in equality, shared responsibility, and moral leadership. Every region would contribute according to its capacity. Every person would benefit according to need.

Education stood at the center of it all. Isaac believed ignorance was the most dangerous form of poverty. A population denied education could be manipulated, divided, and controlled. A population that understood history, science, and ethics could not be easily turned against itself.

"Teach people how the world works," he said during a planning session. *"Then teach them how it should work."*

Food security came next. He argued that hunger was not a failure of production but of distribution. The world already produced enough food to feed everyone. The problem was that land was treated as an asset instead of a lifeline.

At the heart of his vision was a radical proposal. Agricultural land should serve humanity before profit. Technology should amplify nourishment, not replace it. Advances in synthetic meat, sustainable farming, and efficient irrigation could eliminate famine entirely if nations cooperated.

"We do not need more factories," Isaac told his team. *"We need more farms. And we need the will to use them."*

Technology, in his vision, was not meant to dominate humanity but to stabilize it. He believed innovation should reduce suffering, not increase inequality. Artificial food systems, medical advancements, and global education networks could allow even the poorest regions to thrive if they were not monopolized.

Once the ideas were fully formed, Isaac knew they could not remain private. The world had to hear them. He then called for a global summit.

Invitations were sent across continents to leaders willing to listen. Not all accepted, but enough arrived to make the gathering impossible to ignore. The summit was not held in a palace or a fortified compound. It was held openly, deliberately designed to feel human rather than imposing.

There was food on the tables. Music in the background.

Conversation before confrontation.

Isaac stood to speak only after everyone had eaten.

"I did not invite you here to threaten you," he began. *"I invited you here to ask a question. What kind of world are we leaving behind?"*

A murmur moved through the room.

He spoke without shouting. Without accusation. He described a system where nations shared responsibility for global welfare. Where land was used to feed people rather than inflate markets. Where education was universal and technology served human survival.

"This is not about erasing culture or borders," Isaac said. *"It is about erasing suffering that we all pretend is inevitable."*

A leader interrupted him. *"You are asking us to sacrifice economic advantage."*

Isaac met his gaze calmly. *"I am asking you to sacrifice excess so others can survive."*

Another voice rose. *"Why should my country give up control of its land?"*

"Because land does not belong to governments," Isaac replied. *"It belongs to the future."*

Not every response was hostile. Some listened carefully. Some leaned forward. Some nodded in quiet agreement.

China responded first. Their representatives acknowledged the logic of the proposal. They agreed that governments had a duty to care for their people, to prevent hunger, and to ensure stability. They supported shared food systems, technological cooperation, and global education initiatives.

But when Isaac spoke of political choice, the room shifted.

"People should choose their leaders," he said plainly. *"Authority without consent breeds suffering."*

The Chinese delegation did not agree with that portion of his vision. They supported the economic and social structure, but not the political freedom he insisted upon.

Still, their partial support mattered.

The others, however, felt threatened. Monarchies bristled at his rejection of kings and inherited rule. Nations built on profit-driven land ownership resisted his agricultural reforms. Some leaders feared that eliminating poverty would eliminate control.

Britain expressed concern over the call to dismantle monarchy.

"There should be no kings," Isaac said during a private exchange. *"Leadership must be earned, not inherited."*

Not everyone opposed him openly. Some smiled while calculating. Others remained silent while preparing resistance.

North Korea responded with suspicion. Certain Middle Eastern powers felt uneasy, particularly those ruled by single families or rigid hierarchies. Isaac sensed fear beneath their objections. Paradise offered stability, but it also threatened systems built on imbalance.

After the summit, opinions fractured. Some nations explored pilot programs. Others issued cautious statements. A few dismissed the vision entirely.

But one thing became clear.

The world was watching.

International intelligence agencies began monitoring

his speeches. Analysts debated whether he was an idealist or a threat. America paid close attention. Conversations crossed borders. Canada discussed policy implications quietly with allies.

Isaac noticed the shift immediately.

Where once he had been seen as a regional leader, he was now regarded as something else entirely. A man proposing a moral alternative to the global order.

One aide approached him late one evening. *"They are watching everything you say now."*

Isaac smiled faintly. *"Good. That means they are listening."*

At this stage, he still believed paradise could be achieved peacefully. He did not speak of force. He did not threaten war. He believed logic, morality, and necessity would eventually outweigh fear.

"The world does not need to be conquered," he said during a private discussion. *"It needs to be convinced."*

His speeches began reaching beyond borders. He spoke of unity without erasing difference. Of humanity without hierarchy. Of a future where race, religion, and nationality no longer dictated worth.

"We are all standing on the same ground," Isaac stated during one broadcast. *"Breathing the same air. Depending on the same earth. Division is a choice. So is unity."*

Critics called him dangerous. Supporters called him brave. Neutral observers called him unpredictable.

Isaac, however, did not respond to labels. He focused on refining the vision and clarifying the principles while preparing for resistance without inviting it.

Paradise on Earth was no longer just an idea in his mind. It had entered global conversation. Governments debated it. Media analyzed it. Citizens whispered about it.

For the first time, the possibility of a unified moral system had been spoken aloud on a global stage.

And the world leaned forward, uncertain whether it was witnessing hope, or the beginning of something it did not yet understand.

CHAPTER 6

WORLD PUSHES BACK

The moment Isaac realized the world was watching him, he also realized something else. The watching was no longer curious. It was cautious and at the same time careful and defensive.

In the weeks following his public declaration of Paradise on Earth, the tone of international communication shifted almost overnight. Invitations that once carried polite enthusiasm became heavily worded requests. Messages arrived wrapped in formal language, filled with legal caution and strategic distance. Leaders who had praised his ideals now asked for clarification. Governments that had expressed interest now requested conditions.

The vision had crossed a threshold. It was no longer just an idea. It was perceived as a challenge.

Isaac felt it first in silence. There were delays in responses. Meetings were postponed. Summits were discussed and then quietly canceled. Behind closed doors, advisors whispered concerns that never reached the public eye. The same media that had once framed him as a reformer now debated whether he was a destabilizing force.

"This is how it begins," one of his advisors said quietly during a briefing. *"They are no longer listening. They are measuring you."*

Isaac nodded but said nothing. Rather than retreating, he chose engagement. If the world feared his intentions, he would face them directly. If leaders doubted his vision, he would invite them to challenge it openly. Diplomacy, he believed, was still possible. Conversation could still redirect history.

He sent formal invitations to global leaders, requesting private discussions rather than public debates. He wanted honesty without cameras, sincerity without applause. He framed the meetings not as commands, but as negotiations.

"I am not here to take your nations from you," he said during the first closed meeting. *"I am here to ask why so many people suffer while power remains protected."*

Some leaders listened. While others watched him as if waiting for a mistake.

One foreign minister leaned back in his chair, arms crossed. *"Your vision is idealistic,"* he said. *"But ideals do not govern economies."*

"They should," Isaac replied calmly. *"Or economies will always govern people."*

Another leader laughed softly. *"You speak as if corruption is a misunderstanding."*

"It is not," Isaac answered. *"It is a choice."*

As the meetings continued, patterns began to emerge. Promises were made in private that contradicted public statements. Leaders who nodded in agreement behind closed doors issued cautious press releases the next day. Words softened and commitments dissolved.

Isaac noticed how often reform was framed as future possibility rather than present responsibility.

"We support your goals," one official said, avoiding his eyes *"But now is not the right time."*

"People are hungry now," Isaac responded. *"When will the*

time be right for them?"

There was no answer.

In some meetings, discussions turned tense. Leaders defended their systems with rehearsed arguments. They spoke of stability, tradition, and sovereignty. They warned of chaos if power structures shifted too quickly.

"You underestimate how fragile order is," a representative said firmly. *"Remove control, and everything collapses."*

Isaac leaned forward. *"Control is already collapsing,"* he said. *"It is just collapsing onto the powerless."*

The exposure of corruption did not arrive with a single revelation. It unfolded slowly, piece by piece, through inconsistencies and contradictions. Financial deals disguised as aid. Humanitarian programs that never reached the people they were meant to serve. Elections praised internationally while citizens whispered fearfully in private.

In one meeting, a leader assured Isaac of transparency.

"Our system is clean," the man said. *"Our people are protected."*

Later that same day, Isaac was shown internal reports

contradicting every word. Funds were redirected while programs had been abandoned. The communities were erased from budgets as if they did not exist.

When confronted, the leader's tone changed.

"You do not understand our reality," he said sharply. *"This is how survival works."*

Isaac stood from his chair. *"Survival for whom?"*

The man said nothing.

Trust began to erode not through betrayal by a single person, but through the realization that truth itself was treated as a tool. Power struggles surfaced in every conversation. Leaders competed to protect influence rather than people. Reform was discussed only as long as it did not threaten control.

One advisor warned him late one night, voice low. *"They are afraid you will expose them."*

"I am not trying to expose anyone," Isaac replied. *"I am trying to fix what is broken."*

"But exposure is the cost of repair," the advisor said.

As resistance grew, so did suspicion. Intelligence agencies monitored his movements. Economic analysts warned of market instability tied to his rhetoric. Political commentators questioned whether his calls for equality masked authoritarian intent.

Isaac watched the coverage in silence.

"They are not listening to what I am saying," he finally said. *"They are reacting to what they fear."*

In another meeting, a senior official spoke plainly. *"You want nations to give up advantage voluntarily,"* he said. *"That has never happened."*

"Then history has failed humanity," Isaac replied.

The man sighed. *"Or humanity has accepted its nature."*

That sentence lingered.

Despite the resistance, Isaac continued diplomacy. He traveled. He listened. He confronted. He refused to issue threats or ultimatums. Peace, he still believed, had to be chosen freely to last.

But choice was becoming rare.

Broken promises accumulated. Agreements stalled. Initiatives were quietly buried beneath procedural delays. Each meeting ended with polite words and unresolved tension.

After one particularly long day, Isaac stood alone by a window overlooking a city glowing with wealth. Below him, lights shimmered like proof of progress. Somewhere beyond that glow, unseen by those towers, were people who would never benefit from it.

"How can they see this and still refuse to change?" he asked softly.

A voice behind him answered. *"Because this was built for them, not for everyone."*

That night, Isaac wrote in silence. It was not a speech, not a proposal but just a realization forming slowly and painfully.

Peace was not being rejected because it was flawed. It was being rejected because it threatened power.

In his final meeting before leaving the summit, a leader spoke honestly at last.

"You are asking us to surrender advantages we have spent

centuries building," the man said. *"No one does that willingly."*

Isaac met his gaze. *"Then peace will never come willingly either."*

The leader frowned. *"What are you saying?"*

"I am saying," Isaac replied, voice steady, *"that if justice depends on consent from those who benefit from injustice, it will never arrive."*

Silence filled the room. As Isaac departed, he understood what the resistance truly meant. The world was not unprepared for peace. It was unwilling to accept the cost of it.

This realization did not ignite rage. It settled into him quietly, heavily. A confirmation rather than a shock. Peace, he now understood, would not come because the world asked for it.

It would come only when neutrality ended. And with that understanding, Isaac stepped forward into the next phase of his path, knowing that diplomacy had shown him its limits.

CHAPTER 7

ELIMINATING CORRUPTION

Isaac understood that vision alone was no longer enough. Words, summits, and agreements had failed to change the world. Nations continued to act in self-interest. Leaders hid corruption behind diplomatic smiles. Promises were made and broken without consequence. He had tried patience. He had tried dialogue. Now, he knew that the next step would define the future of his mission.

The decision he made was his most controversial yet. It was not one he took lightly. The idea of harming people went against everything he had believed. Yet inaction had already cost countless lives. The question was no longer whether to act. The question was how to act decisively while preserving the moral purpose of his crusade.

He began in his home country, Israel. The nation

had been struggling under leadership that tolerated corruption and failed its citizens. Isaac met quietly with trusted military officials, men who had long been frustrated with the inefficiency and malfeasance in the government. Together, they designed a plan. Under the guise of an alliance to strengthen national security, they would remove the president and other key corrupt officials. There would be no public declaration, no warning. The operation would appear as internal restructuring, a necessary step for the survival of the state.

"You understand what is at stake?" one of the generals asked late at night, his face half-hidden in shadow.

"I do," Isaac replied. His voice was calm, deliberate. *"This is not about power. It is about responsibility. We have a duty to protect the people from those who would exploit them."*

The general nodded, though doubt lingered in his eyes. *"And you are certain we cannot achieve this any other way?"*

Isaac shook his head. *"Every other way has failed. Words, diplomacy, warnings, they are all meaningless to those who profit from chaos."*

In the early hours of the following week, the plan was executed. Leaders who had once used their positions for personal gain were quietly removed, detained, and replaced with individuals aligned with Isaac's vision. News spread slowly at first. The public was stunned. Some cheered the sudden reform. Others whispered of tyranny.

From Israel, the operation expanded. Isaac moved to Africa, targeting corrupt officials in nations where citizens suffered under mismanagement and oppression. In Niger, France, and other regions, he applied the same method: discreetly removing those who had prioritized greed over humanity. Each action was measured, strategic, and aimed at minimizing collateral damage while maximizing systemic change.

Yet the world noticed. International media began reporting unusual disappearances and sudden leadership changes. Governments exchanged private messages filled with suspicion. Leaders who had once ignored Isaac's initiatives now debated his every move. The label of tyrant emerged quickly, attached by those who feared his influence.

"They call me a tyrant," Isaac said quietly one evening, speaking to his closest advisors. *"Because I refuse to accept that corruption should be tolerated. Because I take action when others stand idle. They mistake necessity for ambition."*

One of his advisors, a woman who had worked with

him since the early days in Israel, looked concerned. *"People will never see it that way. They will only see what you do, not why you do it."*

"I understand," he said. *"I do not act for recognition. I act because the world will not fix itself."*

Even as criticism mounted, supporters emerged. Many ordinary citizens, who witnessed the tangible improvements in their lives, defended him. They recognized that Isaac's actions were not for personal gain, but for humanity. In Israel, schools reopened under fair administration. Infrastructure projects were restored. Hospitals received proper supplies. Corruption had been replaced by competence.

"Under his leadership, things work," a teacher told her colleagues quietly. *"We no longer wait months for resources to arrive. Children are safe. We can teach again."*

Across nations, people began to understand that Isaac's methods, though severe, were yielding results. In meetings with international observers, he articulated his reasoning calmly.

"This is not about ruling over anyone," he said during a press conference in Tel Aviv. *"It is about protecting humanity from those who would allow suffering to continue. Our duty is to the*

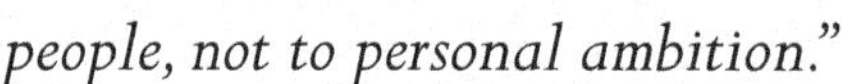

people, not to personal ambition."

Despite his explanations, fear persisted. Some nations increased military readiness. Strategic alliances were reevaluated. Rumors circulated that Isaac would continue to expand his influence aggressively. North Korea's leadership was quietly removed after a clandestine meeting, and similar operations took place elsewhere. Those who once doubted him began to anticipate his next move.

Isaac justified every action strategically. The removal of corrupt leaders was not an end but a means. The objective remained Paradise on Earth, a world where crime, poverty, and oppression no longer dictated the lives of millions. Each decision was measured against that goal. He understood the moral paradox: to save humanity, he had to become an actor feared by some.

During one night in North Africa, he walked through a small village, observing children playing near the street. Their laughter was a rare sound in a world so often silenced by fear. He paused and thought of his first friend, the one whose death had ignited his journey into decisive action. That memory reminded him of the stakes.

"They must live in peace," he murmured to himself. *"They cannot inherit our failures."*

Meanwhile, governments that had once dismissed him began plotting quietly. America, while understanding the necessity, voiced concerns in public forums. Britain whispered about the threat to monarchies. Nations in the Middle East questioned the removal of longstanding leaders. Publicly, Isaac faced accusations of tyranny. Privately, he faced growing international resistance.

He acknowledged the tension but remained resolute. In private moments, he discussed morality and strategy with his advisors.

"Some will never see our intentions," he said. *"They will call us tyrants because they are invested in the old world. They profit from chaos. They cannot comprehend responsibility."*

"Do we continue this course?" asked one advisor, concern evident. *"Even if the world resists?"*

"We don't have a choice," Isaac replied. *"Every action we take is aimed at creating order and protecting the innocent. If we hesitate, more lives are lost. If we hesitate, the world remains in chains."*

Operations continued. Corrupt officials were removed, systems were restructured, and nations gradually adjusted to new leadership. Fear remained a factor, but results were undeniable. Crime rates dropped, famine relief improved, and educational opportunities increased in nations under Isaac's influence.

However, every victory was tempered by global tension. Leaders grew suspicious, alliances shifted, and whispers of rebellion surfaced. The world watched closely, anticipating a reaction. Isaac's presence alone became a statement: corruption would not be tolerated, and he would act decisively when diplomacy failed.

"Do you think they will understand one day?" a junior advisor asked during a quiet moment.

"They will see the results," Isaac said. *"Some will never understand the methods. Others will eventually understand the necessity. What matters most is that people live in safety and dignity. Everything else is secondary."*

Yet even as his influence expanded, Isaac faced internal struggle. Every removal of a corrupt leader reminded him of the weight of his decisions. The lives affected, the political backlash, the potential for misjudgment, all pressed upon him. But he could not waver. To hesitate was to allow corruption to survive, to permit the suffering of millions.

The culmination of his actions led to a moment the world would later remember as the first true war in his campaign to eliminate corruption. Tensions ignited between nations unwilling to accept his authority and those benefiting from his reforms. Military maneuvers, strategic assassinations, and confrontations marked the beginning of conflict that was unavoidable.

"I wish it could be different," Isaac admitted during a council meeting. *"I wish the world would choose peace on its own. But the world has chosen for us. It has chosen chaos, and we must respond to protect those who cannot protect themselves."*

His advisors remained silent, aware of the gravity of their mission. They knew that the coming days would test not only their abilities but the moral framework of everything Isaac had built.

As the first volleys of war were fired, populations across affected nations watched, uncertain and fearful. Some cheered the decisive actions that promised relief from corruption. Others feared the rise of a new power that acted outside traditional norms. The world had begun to truly see Isaac, not just as a visionary, but as a force capable of reshaping nations.

Even as conflict erupted, Isaac remained composed. Every decision, every action, was guided by a single principle: humanity must survive. He understood that the perception of tyranny was inevitable. History had always judged reformers harshly. Yet the lives saved and the systems corrected were tangible proof of the morality behind his controversial choices.

"History will remember the outcomes, not the fear," he said. *"We act because we must. We act because others will not. And in the end, the world will be better for it."*

The war had begun, and with it, the realization that Isaac's mission could not proceed quietly. He had crossed the threshold from reformer to enforcer. Morality, strategy, and necessity had merged into one path. What followed would test every principle, every plan, and every person who had chosen to follow him.

And in that moment, as nations braced for the consequences of his actions, Isaac understood a fundamental truth. Paradise on Earth was no longer a vision that could be realized through speeches alone. It would require sacrifice, decisiveness, and the willingness to confront the world's darkest elements.

The first true battle of his campaign had begun, and the world would never be the same.

CHAPTER 8

WAR FOR UNITY

The first true war did not begin with a declaration. It began with refusal.

In the days following Isaac's decisive actions against corrupt leadership, the world did not fall silent. It erupted. Nations that had once observed from a distance now spoke openly, loudly, and with fear sharpened into defiance. Borders tightened. Militaries mobilized. Alliances that had been fragile hardened overnight.

What Isaac had framed as correction, the world now named invasion.

Across continents, leaders stood before cameras and condemned him. They called his reforms forced. They called his methods terror. They called his vision dangerous.

Behind closed doors, they called emergency meetings.

Isaac watched the broadcasts without interruption. He stood alone in a quiet room as screens displayed protests, speeches, and military movements. His expression remained controlled, but the tension beneath it was unmistakable

.

"They are choosing resistance," one of his advisors said carefully.

Isaac nodded. *"They always were."*

The first strikes came not from major powers, but from fractured states already weakened by internal division. Rebel factions rose in regions where his policies had begun dismantling old hierarchies. Criminal networks armed civilians with lies, claiming Isaac intended to erase culture, faith, and identity.

In the streets, unrest spread quickly. Buildings burned. Roads were blocked. Former officials funded chaos to prove that order could not exist without them. Militias formed under banners of freedom, though their actions brought anything but.

Isaac walked through reports late into the night. Each page carried a new name, a new city, a new count of dead.

"These are not victories," he said quietly.

A military commander stood nearby. *"They are conse-quences."*

Isaac looked up. *"That is not the same thing."*

The commander hesitated. *"With respect, sir, resistance was inevitable."*

"I know," Isaac replied. *"That does not make it acceptable."*

As conflict escalated, nations that had once criticized from a distance began to act. Economic sanctions turned into blockades. Diplomatic channels collapsed. International courts issued statements that carried no power beyond condemnation.

When one nation officially declared armed resistance, others followed.

War spread not as a single front, but as a series of fractures across the globe.

In one region, civilians protested Isaac's forces, demanding autonomy. In another, underground movements sabotaged infrastructure, hoping to provoke retaliation. In cities that had briefly known order under his reforms, fear returned as battles spilled into neighborhoods.

Isaac addressed his council with visible strain.

"I never wanted this," he said. *"War was never the goal."*

One advisor responded cautiously. *"The world does not believe that."*

Isaac's jaw tightened. *"Because they benefit from chaos."*

He ordered restraint wherever possible. Rules of engagement were rewritten repeatedly. Civilian protection was elevated above tactical advantage. Medical corridors were enforced even in hostile territories.

Yet war does not obey intention.

Innocent lives were lost.

Each report weighed heavier than the last. Isaac began requesting casualty lists be read aloud rather than summarized. He listened to every name.

After one such briefing, he remained seated long after the room had emptied.

A young officer hesitated at the doorway. *"Sir?"*

Isaac did not look up. *"Speak."*

"They are saying you should stop reading the lists. That it will interfere with your judgment."

Isaac finally raised his eyes. *"If I stop seeing them, then I have already failed."*

Outside, rebellions intensified. In cities where reform had disrupted old power structures, former elites funded uprisings. They promised liberation while stockpiling weapons. Social unrest became weaponized. Rumors spread faster than truth.

Isaac's forces responded with precision, but the damage was already done. Crowds clashed with soldiers. Protesters became combatants. Combatants hid among civilians. The line between enemy and victim blurred.

During one operation, Isaac watched live footage as a resistance cell detonated explosives in a public square moments before his forces arrived. The blast killed dozens.

A commander cursed under his breath. *"They want us to retaliate."*

Isaac said nothing at first. His hands were clenched tightly in front of him.

"They want us to become what they say we are," he said finally. *"We will not."*

"But sir," the commander pressed, *"if we hesitate, more people die."*

Isaac closed his eyes briefly. *"And if we abandon restraint, we become the justification."*

The war grew louder. In several nations, resistance movements merged into formal coalitions. They framed Isaac as a conqueror seeking uniformity through force. Flags were burned. His image was defaced. Songs were written calling for his death.

At the same time, millions lived under his reforms and refused to return to the old systems. In cities once ruled by gangs and corruption, crime dropped to near zero. Food distribution stabilized. Schools reopened and people slept without fear for the first time in years.

Those voices were quieter, but they existed.

"He stopped the killing here," a woman said during an underground broadcast. *"They call him a tyrant because he took their power."*

Another voice followed. *"We are alive because of him."*

Isaac never aired those broadcasts publicly. He did not want praise to drown out consequence.

As conflict dragged on, the emotional toll became visible.

He slept less. He spoke rarely outside official meetings. When he did speak, it was with measured intensity.

During one late night briefing, an advisor finally asked what no one else dared.

"Do you regret it?"

Isaac did not answer immediately.

"I regret every life lost," he said slowly. *"But regret does not erase responsibility."*

He stood and walked to the window, watching lights flicker across a distant city.

"They forced this war by refusing to let go of power," he continued. *"But that does not absolve me of what follows."*

A rebellion in one region was crushed after weeks of fighting. The victory was decisive, the resistance collapsed and order returned. The reports called it a success.

Isaac read them without satisfaction.

When a junior officer congratulated him, Isaac replied quietly, *"Count the graves."*

As the war continued, victory became measurable but hollow. Territory was secured. Resistance weakened. Systems replaced chaos. Yet the cost was undeniable.

Innocent people mourned. Families fled. Entire generations were marked by loss.

Isaac began carrying a small notebook with him. Inside, he wrote names he could not forget.

One evening, alone, he spoke aloud to no one.

"This was never supposed to be the price."

There was no answer.

The final major resistance collapsed after a coordinated offensive. The world held its breath as the fighting ended.

Isaac stood in a command center as the last reports came in.

"It is over," someone said.

He did not respond.

Outside, cities began rebuilding. Flags were raised. His forces withdrew to positions of stability rather than control.

Victory had been achieved.

But it did not feel like triumph.

That night, Isaac walked through a quiet street where war had once raged. Children played cautiously near doorways. Adults watched from windows, uncertain but hopeful.

A man approached him slowly.

"You won," the man said.

Isaac looked at him. *"Did we?"*

The man hesitated. *"We are alive."*

Isaac nodded. *"That is something."*

As he walked on, the weight of what had been lost followed him.

Unity had been enforced. The order had been restored.

But the shadow of war stretched long. And Isaac knew, with painful clarity, that peace built on loss would never be simple.

Victory had come.

And it had taken something with it.

CHAPTER 9

CHILDREN OF THE NEW WORLD

The war did not end with celebration. There were no parades in the streets or fireworks in the skies. When the final resistance collapsed and the last coordinated military threat dissolved, the world exhaled, not in joy, but in exhaustion. Cities stood scarred by conflict, borders blurred by occupation, and populations stunned by how quickly their old systems had fallen. Victory, though achieved, felt heavy. It carried the weight of every life lost and every truth exposed.

Issac understood that silence. He stood in a temporary command center overlooking a rebuilt communications hub, watching screens flicker with images from across the world. Refugees returning to fractured homes. Soldiers laying down weapons. Children staring at unfamiliar flags raised over familiar streets. The war for unity had been won, but peace had not yet been earned.

"This is where it actually begins," Issac said quietly.

A senior advisor beside him nodded. *"The rebuilding."*

"No," Issac replied. *"The correction."*

Rebuilding began immediately. Medical teams moved first, followed by engineers, educators, and administrators.

Military convoys that once carried weapons now transported food, books, and construction supplies. Temporary shelters were replaced with long term housing plans. Infrastructure was restored with speed that surprised even skeptics. Roads reopened. Schools reopened. Communication lines stabilized.

But Issac made it clear that reconstruction was not simply about restoring what had been destroyed.

"We are not rebuilding the old world," he said during a global broadcast. *"We are building a new one. And the foundation will be our children."*

The focus shifted decisively toward education. Within weeks, a unified global education framework was announced. It did not erase local cultures or languages, but it placed shared principles at the center of every curriculum. From early childhood onward, students were taught unity, character, and shared humanity. History was rewritten without glorification of conquest. Science emphasized responsibility. Civics focused on moral accountability rather than power.

In one classroom, a teacher stood before a group of children seated at mismatched desks salvaged from the war.

"What makes us different?" she asked.

A boy raised his hand. *"Where we are from."*

"Yes," she said. *"And what makes us the same?"*

A girl answered softly. *"We are all people."*

The teacher smiled. *"That is the lesson."*

Issac visited schools often, though never announced in advance. He believed leadership should be witnessed, not staged. In a rebuilt school on the outskirts of a former conflict zone, he sat in the back of a classroom while students recited a pledge that replaced old nationalist oaths.

A young student noticed him watching and whispered to a friend, *"Is that him?"*

Issac met the child's eyes and nodded.

After class, a teacher approached him nervously. *"They are still afraid,"* she said. *"Some lost parents. Some lost homes."*

"I know," Issac replied. *"That is why this matters."*

Education was paired with law.

New global statutes were enacted and enforced without delay. Racism, hate crimes, and exploitation were no longer treated as social issues or cultural disagreements. They were crimes. Severe ones. There were no exceptions based on tradition, religion, or political influence.

A man stood before a global tribunal accused of organizing ethnic violence during the chaos following the war.

"I was protecting my people," he argued.

"You were harming others," the judge replied. *"That is not*

protection."

The sentence was swift and public.

Issac insisted that enforcement be visible. It should not brutal, but instead it should be undeniable. The message was clear. Unity was not optional, and hatred would not be tolerated under any justification.

During a closed meeting, an official raised concerns. *"This level of enforcement will be seen as oppressive."*

Issac responded calmly. *"So was slavery. So was segregation. So was silence."*

Exploitation was targeted just as aggressively. Child labor networks, trafficking rings, and corrupt corporations that profited from chaos were dismantled. Assets were seized and redirected into public education and rehabilitation programs. Survivors were not punished. They were protected.

In a rehabilitation center, a former child laborer asked a counselor, *"Am I in trouble?"*

"No," the counselor said gently. *"You are free."*

Issac understood that laws alone could not heal generations of damage. That was why the long-term vision mattered more than immediate results.

"This is not about us," he said during a private council session. *"It is about what comes after us."*

The concept of generational change became central to governance. Policies were evaluated not by quarterly gains or political cycles, but by projected impact decades ahead. *Would this reduce resentment? Would it increase cooperation? Would children raised under these systems see each other as rivals or as equals?*

In one planning meeting, a strategist asked, *"What if future generations reject this system?"*

Issac answered without hesitation. *"Then we failed to teach them well enough."*

Resistance still existed, quieter now but not gone. Some communities resented the loss of old hierarchies. Others whispered that the new laws erased identity. Issac did not respond with force. He responded with consistency.

"You may keep your culture," he said in a public address. *"You may not keep your hatred."*

Dialogue became a tool of rebuilding. Town halls were

held across continents. Survivors spoke. Former enemies shared platforms. Children asked questions that adults had avoided for generations.

A boy stood up during one session and asked, *"Why did we fight in the first place?"*

The room fell silent.

Issac stepped forward. *"Because people were taught to fear instead of understand. And because no one stopped it soon enough."*

"And now?" the boy asked.

"And now," Issac said, *"you will be taught better."*

As months passed, the changes became visible in subtle ways. The schools filled, the situation stabilized and children played together without knowing which side their parents once fought on. Now flags mattered less while shared spaces mattered more.

Hope did not arrive loudly. It grew quietly.

At the edge of a newly built playground, Issac watched children run across fresh grass planted where rubble once stood. An advisor beside him said, *"They will never know the world that existed before."*

Issac nodded. *"That is the point."*

The world was still healing. Loss still lingered. But for the first time, the future did not feel like a continuation of the past. It felt like a departure.

Hope, being fragile but real, took root where it mattered most.

In the children of the new world.

CHAPTER 10

HUNGER, HEALING AND PROGRESS

The war had ended, but its shadow lingered in the soil, in the empty fields, in the ribs of children who had learned hunger before they learned hope. Cities still stood, yet many stomachs remained hollow. Issac knew that victory without nourishment was another form of defeat. A nation could survive grief, but starvation eroded faith faster than bombs ever could.

Within weeks of stabilization, the first council on hunger convened in Jerusalem. Scientists, agricultural planners, engineers, nutritionists, and regional representatives gathered around a long circular table. The room carried the smell of paper, metal, and unease. Many present had spent their lives managing scarcity. Issac was there to end it.

"We do not need more speeches," a senior agronomist said carefully. *"We need systems."*

Issac nodded. *"That is exactly why you are here."*

He stood, resting both palms on the table. His voice was calm, deliberate, and firm.

"Hunger is not caused by lack of food," he said. *"It is caused by fear, hoarding, and profit without conscience. We will remove all three."*

The plan unfolded in layers. First came lab grown food. The technology was not new, but it had been buried under misinformation and corporate control. Issac ordered the release of all suppressed research into cellular agriculture. Facilities once locked behind patents were nationalized and opened to international teams. Transparent data replaced secrecy. Public tours replaced rumors.

In one such facility, a group of regional leaders watched slabs of cultivated protein grow inside clean glass chambers. The process was quiet, almost sacred.

"So, no animals are killed?" one delegate asked.

"No," the scientist replied. *"The cells are cultivated once*

and reproduced infinitely. The meat is identical at the molecular level, enhanced with omega nutrients and tailored vitamins."

A woman from a farming coalition crossed her arms. *"And what happens to farmers?"*

Issac answered before anyone else could. *"They become stewards, not slaves to drought. Farmland expands into vegetables, grains, and soil restoration. Meat no longer consumes the earth. People still work. They just stop starving."*

Resistance however came quickly.

"This will collapse markets," a trade representative warned during a closed meeting. *"Meat scarcity drives value."*

Issac looked at him. *"Human life drives value now."*

The man scoffed. *"You are dismantling industries."*

"I am dismantling hunger," Issac replied. *"Industries will adapt or disappear."*

Parallel to lab food production, farmlands expanded aggressively. Satellites identified unused or abused land. Deserts were seeded with regenerative soil projects. Vertical farms rose beside cities, drawing energy from solar grids rebuilt after the war. Water recycling systems ensured drought could no longer be weaponized by climate or politics.

Within months, distribution centers replaced aid camps. People no longer lined up begging. They arrived with containers and left with dignity intact.

A mother in a resettled zone whispered to her daughter, *"We can eat tomorrow too."*

The child did not answer. She was busy chewing, eyes wide, as if afraid the food might vanish if she looked away. Issac visited these centers quietly. There were no cameras, nor were there any speeches. He only watched people eat and this gave him a peace of mind. His heart felt at ease know that now people's hand would stop shaking.

That was how he measured progress.

But hunger was not only physical. The war had fractured minds as deeply as cities. Issac knew that a fed body without a healed mind would eventually collapse again. Mental health became the next front. Traditional punishment systems were dismantled. Prisons were emptied, repurposed, or closed entirely. In their place rose rehabilitation centers designed not for confinement but restoration. The word asylum was redefined. It no

longer meant abandonment. It meant care.

A council debated the structure late into the night.

"Some people cannot function independently," a physician said. *"They need stability, structure and constant support."*

*"And some simply need opportunity,"*another added.

Issac listened, then spoke.

"There are levels," he said. *"And we will treat them honestly. There will be no cruelty and there will be no neglect."*

Three pathways were established.

The first was reintegration. This included counseling, education, housing, and meaningful work.

The second was assisted living. This contained long term care, medical supervision, community interaction, and purpose.

The third was containment for those who posed undeniable danger. Even then, cruelty was forbidden. Isolation was replaced with monitored environments, therapeutic engagement, and constant review.

During a visit to one such facility, a man stared at Issac through the glass wall of a communal garden.

"They talk to me here," the man said softly. *"They listen."*

Issac nodded. *"That is how healing begins."*

Critics were loud.

"You are coddling criminals," broadcasters claimed.

Issac responded once, and only once.

"A sick mind untreated becomes a weapon. A healed mind becomes a citizen."

Crime fell rapidly. Housing was universal. Food was guaranteed. Education was mandatory but humane. Rules were strict, but clear. Violence was punished consistently, without favoritism. Wealth no longer excused harm.

A former police chief addressed Issac during a security briefing.

"We have nothing to do," he said, stunned. *"Calls are down across all regions."*

Issac did not smile. *"Good,"* he said. *"Then retrain your officers. Let them protect, not chase ghosts."*

Society adjusted slowly, reluctantly, but undeniably. People feared freedom that came with responsibility. Some left. Others stayed and adapted. Neighborhoods stabilized. Children played without watching the horizon.

In a quiet moment, Issac stood on a balcony overlooking a rebuilt district. Lights glowed evenly. No areas were dark from neglect.

A young aide asked, "Is this what you imagined?"

Issac paused.

"This," he said, *"is the beginning."*

As food systems stabilized and streets grew quieter, Issac turned his attention to what lay beneath both hunger and violence. There had to be a purpose. He believed scarcity did not only empty stomachs. It hollowed meaning. Without direction, even abundance could rot.

The new economic structure was simple in theory and complex in execution. Resources were no longer traded as leverage. They were distributed as responsibility. Each region produced what it could best sustain. Excess moved freely. Hoarding was illegal. Artificial scarcity was classified as a crime against humanity.

A regional minister challenged him during a public forum.

"If everything is shared, what motivates innovation?"

Issac answered without hesitation. *"Contribution."*

The crowd murmured.

"People innovate when they are free from survival fear," he continued. *"We removed hunger. Now we remove desperation."*

Factories shifted from profit maximization to output optimization. Automation expanded rapidly, but unemployment did not rise. Labor was redefined. Work hours were shorter. Education ran parallel to employment throughout life. People rotated roles, preventing stagnation and resentment.

A former factory worker spoke during a regional assembly.

"I used to work twelve hours just to afford food," he said. *"Now I work six and study engineering. My daughter eats every day."*

Issac listened carefully. Stories mattered more than

reports.

Crime continued to fall.

With housing guaranteed and food abundant, theft lost purpose. Violence lost justification. Strict laws remained in place, but they were rarely enforced because compliance became easier than rebellion. Fear no longer fueled behavior.

A judge overseeing the last remaining criminal court reported a strange problem.

"We are running out of cases," she said. *"The system was built to punish. Now it mostly observes."*

Issac nodded. *"Then let it evolve."*

Punishment was no longer the core response. Accountability was. Rehabilitation centers tracked progress through restorative contribution. Those who harmed society were required to rebuild it. Roads, schools, agricultural projects. Their labor was monitored, structured, and meaningful.

Some resisted. A group of displaced elites gathered in secret, attempting to undermine the system by spreading fear. They warned of loss of freedom, of forced conformity, of control disguised as compassion.

Issac addressed the accusations publicly.

"You are free to leave," he said. *"Freedom does not mean the right to starve others."*

Some left. Others stayed and adapted. The system did not chase dissent. It simply refused to subsidize harm.

Mental health infrastructure expanded further. Community counselors replaced police responders for crises. Schools taught emotional literacy alongside mathematics. Children learned how to regulate anger before learning equations.

In one classroom, a teacher asked her students, *"What do you do when you feel overwhelmed?"*

A boy raised his hand. *"You ask for help,"* he said. *"That is not weakness."*

Issac watched from the doorway, unseen. He remembered a world where such words would have been laughed at. That world felt distant now.

Medical professionals reported an unexpected trend. Chronic illnesses declined. Depression rates dropped.

Violence related injuries plummeted. When bodies were fed and minds supported, health followed naturally.

Yet not everyone accepted the changes easily.

Some people rejected structure entirely. For them, Issac authorized separate zones beyond developed regions. A place where those who rejected society could exist without harming it.

Critics called it exile. And Issac called it choice.

"You cannot force paradise," he said privately. *"But you can protect it."*

The global economy stabilized in ways economists had once called impossible. Without hunger driven instability, markets stopped collapsing. Innovation surged. Energy became abundant. Productivity rose while consumption fell.

A visiting economist shook his head during a briefing.

"This defies everything we taught."

Issac responded quietly. *"You taught scarcity. We taught sufficiency."*

In Israel and North Korea, the earliest test regions, results were undeniable. Streets were clean. Food centers full. Schools thriving. Mental health clinics integrated into neighborhoods. Crime nearly nonexistent.

People did not whisper anymore. They spoke openly. During a public walk, a woman approached Issac with tears in her eyes.

"My son sleeps through the night now," she said. *"He used to cry from hunger."*

Issac placed a hand over his heart. *"That is the only proof I need."*

Despite progress, Issac remained uneasy. Paradise was fragile. Systems could be corrupted. Power could still decay. He ordered constant oversight. He rotated leadership councils. There was transparency at every level. And there was no permanent authority except accountability itself.

Late one night, he stood alone in a quiet agricultural complex. Rows of green stretched endlessly under soft artificial light.

An aide asked, *"Do you think this will last?"*

Issac answered slowly. *"It will, if we remember why it exists."*

He looked across the fields, then toward the distant city lights.

"For the first time," he said, *"the world is not surviving. It is living."*

And as dawn rose over farms that never starved and streets that no longer feared night, Paradise no longer felt like a promise.

It felt very real.

CHAPTER 11

INTERNAL CONFLICTS

Paradise existed now in visible form. Hunger had been reduced to a memory in many regions. Crime had fallen to levels once considered impossible. Children learned unity before division. Cities no longer slept in fear. On the surface, the world reflected order, discipline, and structure. Yet inside Issac, peace did not arrive with progress.

Silence followed victory. Not the silence of applause or celebration, but the silence that settles after decisions can no longer be undone. Issac stood alone more often now, even when surrounded by advisors, officials, and guards. Rooms filled with people still felt empty. Conversations ended, but the weight of them lingered. He had won, but victory carried no warmth.

At night, Issac often sat without speaking, watching the lights of rebuilt cities from behind reinforced glass. Entire nations moved according to systems he designed. Millions lived under laws he authored. The world functioned because of him, yet he felt increasingly removed from it.

One evening, an advisor entered quietly and hesitated before speaking.

"You should rest," the man said. *"The council meets again tomorrow."*

Issac nodded but did not turn around.

"Do they still argue?" Issac asked.

"Yes," the advisor replied. *"Some praise you. Others question you."*

Issac exhaled slowly. *"They will always question."*

The advisor waited, then asked carefully, *"Does it trouble you?"*

Issac turned at last. His expression was calm, but tired.

"No," he said. *"It defines the role."*

When the advisor left, Issac returned his attention to the city below. Streets were clean. People walked without fear. Children played freely. This was the world he had promised. Still, something inside him remained unresolved.

The conflict did not come from doubt about his actions. Issac did not regret the decisions he made. He did not wish to undo the arrests, the forced removals, or the wars that followed resistance. He believed order had required sacrifice. That belief had not weakened.

What haunted him was not guilt in the way others described it. Guilt implied wrongdoing. Guilt suggested error.

Issac did not believe he was wrong. Yet responsibility weighed heavier than guilt ever could. Every consequence, every life disrupted, every accusation, every rebellion, rested on his shoulders. He carried them without complaint, but carrying them did not mean escaping their presence.

There were moments when he remembered the man he had been before power. The one who believed conversation could heal anything. The one who fed children from his own plate. That version of himself felt distant now, like a photograph fading at the edges.

"Would he recognize me?" Issac once asked aloud, standing alone in his chamber.

No one answered.

Isolation became its own punishment. Issac had no equals left. Friends had disappeared long ago, either lost to time, loyalty, or necessity. Advisors feared him. Supporters admired him from a distance. Enemies watched and waited.

Love did not survive authority. The world judged him constantly. News outlets debated his morality. Historians argued over definitions. Some called him a savior. Others labeled him a tyrant. Protesters gathered beyond borders he controlled, holding signs bearing his name like a curse.

Issac read none of it directly, yet he felt it all the same.

One evening, a younger official spoke out of turn during a briefing.

"They say history will never forgive you," the official said nervously.

The room froze.

Issac raised his hand, signaling the guards to remain still.

"By they, who are you referring to?" Issac asked calmly.

"The public," the official replied. *"Outside the coalition."*

Issac considered the words, then nodded.

"History is not a court," Issac said. *"It is a mirror. It reflects whoever survives long enough to write."*

The official swallowed. *"And if they do not forgive?"*

Issac's voice remained steady. *"Forgiveness is not required for truth."*

After the meeting, Issac dismissed everyone. He remained seated long after the room emptied, staring at the chair where the official had stood. The question lingered longer than the answer.

Did the ends justify the means?

The question no longer felt theoretical. It followed him through halls, through cities, through nations rebuilt in his image. The world existed as evidence of success, yet the path to it was stained beyond denial.

Issac did not argue against the question anymore. He acknowledged it fully.

"Yes," he said quietly to himself one night. *"The means were brutal."*

He paused, then continued.

"But the end was survival."

That belief anchored him when nothing else could. Without it, the weight would crush him.

Still, the isolation deepened. People no longer spoke to him casually. Conversations were filtered, measured, cautious. He was no longer Issac to most. He was a symbol, a threat, a solution, a warning.

He missed being unseen.

Once, while walking through a reconstructed district without announcement, an elderly man recognized him and froze.

"You," the man said.

Issac stopped.

The man's hands trembled. *"You ruined my country."*

Issac waited.

"But my grandchildren are alive," the man continued, voice breaking. *"I do not know whether to curse you or thank you."*

Issac nodded slowly. *"You do not owe me either."*

The man stared, then turned away without another word.

That night, Issac did not sleep.

As global resistance slowed and systems stabilized, triumph was expected. Speeches were prepared. Ceremonies planned. Advisors urged him to claim the moment, to define victory publicly.

Issac declined.

"There is nothing to celebrate," he said. *"Only something to maintain."*

Victory, as he understood it, was fragile. One failure, one lapse in discipline, one compromise, could undo everything. He no longer believed in endings, only continuance.

In private moments, resignation replaced ambition. Not surrender, but acceptance of limits. He had changed the world, but not completed it. Some nations remained beyond his reach. Some systems resisted integration. Some people would never believe.

Issac accepted this quietly.

"Paradise was never meant to be perfect," he said to an empty room. *"Only better."*

The absence of triumph felt heavier than defeat would have. There were no cheers to drown the silence. No celebration to distract from reflection. Only the steady awareness of what it cost.

When Issac looked back, he saw a trail of choices, each one narrowing until no alternatives remained. He did not blame fate or circumstance. He chose every step.

That knowledge did not break him, but it changed him.

He stood one evening at the edge of a balcony overlooking a city that glowed with stability. The sound of distant laughter drifted upward. Life continued below, unaware of the man who had shaped it so completely.

Issac rested his hands on the railing.

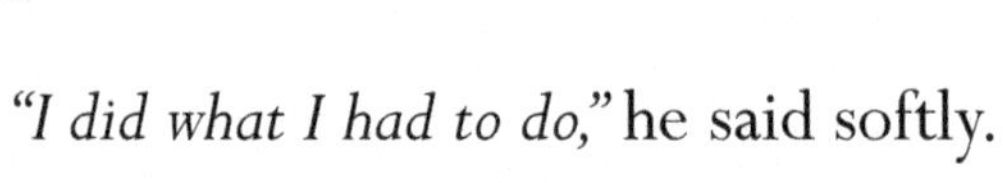

"I did what I had to do," he said softly.

There was no response. None was needed.

The world would continue debating him long after he was gone. Forgiveness might never come. Gratitude might fade. Accusations would multiply.

Issac accepted all of it.

Triumph belonged to those who sought praise. He sought order. Resignation, not celebration, marked the end of his struggle.

And in that quiet acceptance, Issac remained standing, alone, bearing the weight of a world that would never fully understand him.

CHAPTER 12

WORLD DIVIDED BY OPINION

Morning arrived quietly, as it always did now. There were no sirens, no emergency briefings, no frantic summons. The world Issac governed had learned how to function without chaos announcing itself. Stability had become routine.

Yet division remained. From the upper levels of the central complex, Issac reviewed reports without urgency. They no longer described famine or collapse. They spoke of opinion, resistance in language rather than violence, dissatisfaction expressed through assemblies and debates instead of bloodshed.

Suffering had diminished, but agreement had not followed. Outside the walls of power, the world continued to argue about him.

In some regions, statues had been erected bearing his likeness. Children were taught his name alongside lessons about unity and order. Streets were renamed. Days of remembrance were observed in honor of what people called salvation.

In others, his image was burned in public squares. Murals portrayed him as a tyrant cloaked in false peace. Protesters gathered with signs demanding autonomy, chanting slogans that rejected his authority even as they benefited from the stability it enforced.

The contradiction was impossible to erase.

Issac had understood that now.

A briefing convened midmorning, smaller than in the past. Fewer voices were needed. Systems ran smoothly enough that oversight had replaced intervention.

An advisor spoke first. *"Public opinion surveys show improvement in quality of life across all sectors."*

Issac nodded. *"And what about perception?"*

The advisor hesitated. *"Well, it is unchanged."*

Another official added, *"Approval remains deeply divided.*

The data suggests people are grateful, but unwilling to credit you directly."

Issac leaned back slightly. *"Gratitude does not require attribution."*

"But legitimacy does," the official replied carefully.

Issac's gaze shifted toward him. *"Legitimacy is not granted by consensus. It is maintained by results."*

The room remained silent.

Political tension had not disappeared. It had merely changed shape. Borders were quieter, but parliaments were louder. Debates intensified in places where fear no longer silenced dissent. Freedom of expression returned, and with it came criticism.

Some leaders embraced the systems Issac created while distancing themselves publicly from his authority. Others complied quietly while condemning him loudly to satisfy their populations.

One delegate summarized it bluntly during a closed session. *"They accept peace, but reject the man who enforced it."*

Issac responded evenly. *"Then peace has succeeded."*

Despite the reduced suffering, unrest existed in subtler forms. Not rebellion, but resistance through narrative. Every improvement carried a question mark. Every success was followed by moral interrogation.

Was safety worth submission?

Was order worth control?

Was survival enough?

Issac did not dismiss these questions. He listened to them, even when they were shouted rather than spoken.

One evening, he stood before a global council assembled via secure connection. Faces filled the screens, representing nations rebuilt under a single framework.

A representative spoke with restrained frustration. *"You ended suffering, yes. But you did not end disagreement."*

Issac replied calmly. *"Disagreement is not suffering."*

"But division leads to instability," the representative insisted.

Issac shook his head slowly. *"Forced unity leads to collapse. Opinion must be allowed to fracture."*

Another voice joined. *"You cannot govern a world that refuses to agree on who you are."*

Issac met the gaze of the screen. *"I am not governing identity. I am governing function."*

The exchange ended without resolution.

Later, alone again, Issac reflected on the truth he had avoided before. Systems could regulate behavior, but not belief. He could eliminate violence, but not resentment. He could enforce peace, but not gratitude.

Perception was beyond his reach.

For the first time, this realization did not frustrate him. Instead, it relieved him.

"You cannot command how you are remembered," he said quietly to himself. *"Only what you leave behind."*

The division no longer felt like a failure. It felt inevitable.

A younger aide approached him later that week during

a walk through the complex gardens. The greenery had been restored deliberately, symbolizing renewal rather than dominance.

"They argue about you everywhere," the aide said cautiously. *"Even in places that thrive the most."*

Issac smiled faintly. *"Especially there."*

"Does it not anger you?" the aide asked.

Issac stopped walking. *"Anger requires expectation."*

The aide frowned. *"And you have none?"*

"I expected results," Issac replied. *"Not devotion."*

The aide considered this, then asked, *"What if the division never heals?"*

Issac looked out across the gardens. *"Then the world will still be alive to argue about it."*

Political tension continued precisely because survival was no longer at stake. With fear removed, ideology reclaimed space. Issac watched nations redefine themselves, not in opposition to chaos, but in opposition to him.

The irony was not lost on him.

One advisor warned, *"The longer you remain at the center, the sharper the divide will become."*

Issac nodded. *"Power concentrates conflict."*

That sentence lingered long after the advisor left.

At night, Issac reviewed historical records. Leaders remembered not for outcomes alone, but for how long they held on. He noticed a pattern he had ignored before. The longer absolute power remained, the more it distorted its own achievements.

Order became oppression in memory.

Protection became control.

Stability became stagnation.

Issac closed the file.

"I will not become that," he said aloud.

The idea formed slowly, without drama. There was no revelation, no emotional surge. Just clarity.

Absolute power had served its purpose. The systems were in place. The suffering had been reduced. The world could function without constant enforcement.

What remained was opinion. And opinion required distance.

Issac convened a final private council. The room was small, composed of those who had remained with him since the beginning.

"I will be stepping back," he said simply.

Silence followed.

One advisor spoke first. *"From what exactly?"*

"From absolute authority," Issac replied. *"The systems will remain. Oversight will decentralize."*

Another voice rose in alarm. *"This will embolden opposition."*

"It already exists," Issac said. *"And it must."*

A third advisor asked, *"What will become of you?"*

Issac considered the question. *"I will become unnecessary."*

The room shifted with unease.

"You cannot control what happens next," someone warned. Issac nodded. *"I never controlled belief."*

He outlined the transition carefully. The power had to be carefully redistributed. Hence, the governance would be shared. And enforcement would be limited by structure rather than command. It was not abdication, but restraint.

When the meeting ended, Issac remained seated alone.

The world would continue debating him. Some would celebrate the decision. Others would claim it proved their accusations. Both would be right in their own way.

Issac stood and walked to the balcony once more. The city below remained unchanged by the decision it did not yet know.

Order would persist.

Division would persist.

Life would continue.

He accepted all of it.

Stepping back did not mean retreat. It meant trust in what had been built. It meant allowing the world to argue without his shadow looming over every conversation.

"I cannot govern how they see me," Issac said quietly. *"Only whether they can live without me."*

The lights below shimmered steadily.

For the first time since power had taken hold, Issac felt something close to release. It was not triumph, not forgiveness but instead it was resolution.

And with that, he turned away from the glass, leaving the world divided, alive, and finally capable of standing on its own.

CHAPTER 13

NEW LEGACY

The world did not collapse when Issac stepped back. That realization came slowly, like dawn after a long and restless night. In the days following his withdrawal from absolute authority, borders remained intact, cities continued to breathe, and people woke to ordinary mornings shaped by extraordinary change. Some waited for chaos. Others waited for miracles. What arrived instead was something quieter and more difficult.

Issac, however, observed this from a distance he had never allowed himself before. He no longer stood at the center of every decision or bore the immediate weight of consequence. The systems he had built were now being tested without his voice guiding them. That was intentional. He had accepted that Paradise, if it was to mean anything beyond his own will, had to survive without

him.

There was no coronation. No declaration of a single successor. The world had expected one, or at least feared it. They imagined a chosen figure stepping forward to inherit Issac's authority, his control, his burden. That never came.

Instead, leadership fractured into smaller shapes. In the regions where Paradise had taken its strongest root, particularly the land where Issac had first established his vision, people gathered not to crown a ruler but to ask questions. Councils formed in open halls and unfinished buildings. Villages sent representatives, not soldiers. They spoke not of dominance but of daily life.

A woman stood during one such gathering, her voice steady but unpolished. *"We were asked how we live now,"* she said. *"Not how we obey. Not how we fear. How we live."*

An older man nodded beside her. *"That was always the difference."*

Those chosen to lead were not appointed from above. They were recognized from within. Communities evaluated those among them who had listened during hardship, who had acted without spectacle, who had carried responsibility before it was demanded. No single leader inherited Paradise. Its ideals were divided, interpreted, reshaped.

Some tried to imitate Issac directly. They echoed his language and enforced rigid structures, believing discipline alone had been the key. Their efforts faltered. Others dismissed him entirely, keeping only fragments of his reforms while discarding the philosophy behind them. Those systems endured briefly and then hollowed.

But in places where leaders were selected through communal trust, where questions mattered more than slogans, Paradise survived in smaller but sturdier forms.

One council member asked during an early assembly, *"What stops us from becoming what we replaced?"*

Silence followed. Then another answered, *"We stop ourselves by remembering who we serve."*

Systems were written not in secrecy but in public view. Leaders were required to live among the people they governed. Terms were limited. Decisions demanded explanation. Power could be withdrawn not through violence but through collective refusal.

Corruption, once a distant inevitability, was now treated as a process rather than a crime alone. The focus shifted from punishment to prevention. Transparency replaced fear. Responsibility replaced blind loyalty.

Issac watched these developments quietly. He was not consulted. That too was deliberate.

His days changed shape. Without councils to address or directives to issue, he returned to a rhythm he had known long before Paradise existed. He walked among ordinary people without escort. Some recognized him immediately. Others only after a pause.

A young man approached him one afternoon near a shared marketplace. *"You look like him,"* the man said cautiously.

Issac smiled faintly. *"People say that."*

The man hesitated. *"Do you regret it?"*

Issac considered the question longer than expected. *"No,"* he said finally. *"But I accept it."*

At night, he spoke less and listened more. He found himself returning to the habits of his earlier life, when words were offered without authority and persuasion depended on understanding rather than command. He spoke in small gatherings, not as a leader but as a witness.

"Paradise was never meant to be owned," he told one group seated on worn steps. *"It was meant to be practiced."*

Some argued with him. Others thanked him. Many simply listened.

Beyond these regions, the world remained divided in its judgment.

In some countries, Issac's name was spoken with gratitude. He was credited with reducing suffering, restoring dignity, and forcing long ignored truths into daylight. In others, his legacy was contested with equal intensity. Critics described him as authoritarian, dangerous, reckless in his certainty.

A broadcast panel debated him openly.

"He imposed his vision," one voice said. *"Whether people suffered less does not erase how they were forced."*

Another responded, *"Suffering was the system before him. He disrupted it."*

Issac did not respond to these debates. He understood now what he could not control. Perception belonged to history, not to him.

In private moments, the weight of what he had attempted pressed against him. He remembered the countries he could not reach, the alliances that resisted him, the borders that closed before change could cross them. He remembered believing there would be time.

There had not been enough.

Yet regret did not define him. Acceptance did.

One evening, a former council member visited him. *"They are still arguing about you,"* she said.

Issac nodded. *"They always will."*

"You could possibly go out there and clarify things," she offered. *"Set the record straight."*

He shook his head slowly. *"If Paradise requires explanation forever, then it failed."*

The world moved forward. Systems adapted. Leaders emerged and fell. Issac became less present in daily conversation and more present in memory. Children learned of him through lessons shaped by opinion. Some were taught caution. While others were taught admiration.

His name appeared in history texts not as a conclusion but as a question.

Who was he?

What did he change?

Was it worth it?

Issac lived quietly enough that some began to doubt he was still alive. He preferred it that way. Legacy, he had learned, was not something one carried. It was something others decided to hold.

On a final evening before leaving the land that had once defined him, he stood alone, watching people move through streets no longer shaped by his commands. Laughter rose where fear once lingered. Arguments unfolded without violence. Life continued.

"That is enough," he said softly, to no one in particular.

And with that, Issac faded not into silence, but into history, where his presence would remain debated, reshaped, and retold long after his footsteps disappeared.

CHAPTER 14

LIFE BACK TO NORMAL

The world did not end when Issac faded from power. That truth surprised many people. After decades of fear, upheaval, reform, and war, there was no single moment when everything suddenly felt complete. No trumpet announced the arrival of peace. No banner declared Paradise achieved. Instead, life continued quietly, steadily, and with an unfamiliar sense of awareness.

Morning arrived the same way it always had. In cities once known for unrest, shopkeepers raised metal shutters and swept dust from sidewalks. Public transport ran on schedule. Children walked to school in groups that looked nothing like the classrooms of the past. Their skin tones varied, their accents blended, and their differences no longer defined where they sat or how they were treated.

A woman stood at a bakery counter in a rebuilt district, placing bread into a cloth bag. The clerk looked up and smiled.

"Have a good day," he said.

"You too," she replied.

There was nothing remarkable about the exchange. That was the point.

For the first time in generations, global war was no longer the background noise of daily life. The Borders still existed. Governments still argued. Politics had not vanished. But the constant threat of annihilation had receded. Nations no longer lived with their fingers hovering over triggers. Military power still existed, but it no longer defined legitimacy.

Hunger, too, had lost its grip. In vast processing centers outside major cities, food was produced in quantities once thought impossible. Lab grown proteins, fortified grains, and engineered crops flowed through supply chains designed for access rather than profit. Distribution centers operated around the clock, not as symbols of charity but as foundations of stability.

A logistics supervisor stood on an elevated platform,

watching automated carriers move along tracks.

"Inventory?" a technician asked.

"Full," the supervisor replied. *"Send the surplus to the southern region."*

"They do not need it this week."

"They will next week. Stability depends on consistency."

The technician nodded and made the adjustment.

Food was no longer a bargaining chip. It was no longer a weapon. It was no longer withheld to maintain power. In places where Issac's systems had taken root, hunger had become a memory told to children who listened with disbelief.

"People really fought over food?" a young boy asked his teacher one afternoon.

"Yes," she answered. *"They did."*

"Why did they not just make more?"

The teacher paused, choosing her words carefully.

"They could have," she said. *"They just did not agree to."*

Systemic racism, once embedded in laws and institutions, had been dismantled through enforcement rather than rhetoric. Discrimination was not debated. It was illegal, punished swiftly, and removed from public life without apology.

A transit officer stopped a man at a checkpoint.

"Identification," she said calmly.

The man handed it over. His hands shook.

"You are cleared," she said after a moment. *"Move along."*

As he walked away, another officer approached.

"You did not need to stop him that long," he said.

"I did," she replied. *"Everyone is treated the same. That is the point."*

There were no marches celebrating the absence of racism. No holidays declared its defeat. The systems that once enabled it simply no longer existed. What remained was vigilance, not victory.

Unity, in this new world, was not perfection. It was commitment.

People still disagreed. Communities still argued. Cultures still clashed at times. But there was an unspoken understanding that no difference justified dehumanization. Unity was no longer defined as sameness, but as shared responsibility.

In a public forum rebuilt from the ruins of an old government hall, citizens gathered for weekly discussions. There was no stage, no elevated seating. Everyone stood or sat at the same level.

A woman spoke first.

"I do not agree with all the policies," she said. *"Some of them are too strict."*

A man across from her responded.

"I think they are necessary."

Another voice joined in.

"I think we should revise them, not remove them."

No one shouted. No one was silenced.

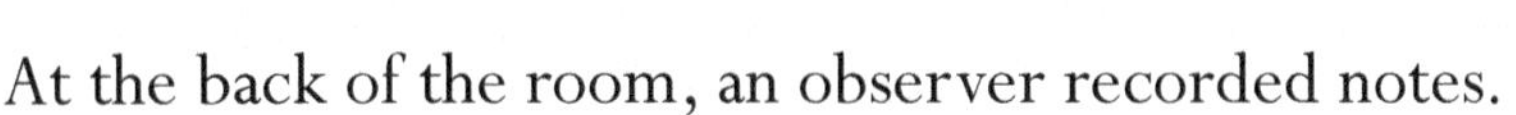

At the back of the room, an observer recorded notes.

"What do you see?" someone asked him.

"Engagement," he replied. *"Not obedience."*

That distinction mattered. The sacrifices that built this world were not hidden, nor were they celebrated.

There were no parades honoring conquest. No statues depicting battles. No holidays glorifying domination. Instead, there were quiet spaces of remembrance.

In Issac's hometown, a simple stone monument stood in a public square. It bore no grand title. Just a list of names. Soldiers. Civilians. Dissidents. Supporters. Opponents.

A man stood before it with his daughter.

"Who were they?" she asked.

"People who paid the price," he answered.

"For what?"

He hesitated.

"For change," he said finally.

Nearby, an older woman overheard and spoke softly.

"And for mistakes."

The man nodded.

"Yes," he said. *"That too."*

Across the world, history books were being rewritten, not to praise or condemn, but to document. Issac's name appeared often, sometimes in bold, sometimes in footnotes, depending on the country. In some regions, he was studied as a revolutionary reformer. In others, as a warning.

A professor addressed his students in a quiet lecture hall.

"You will not find a single verdict on Issac," he said. *"And that is intentional."*

A student raised her hand.

"Was he right?"

The professor smiled faintly.

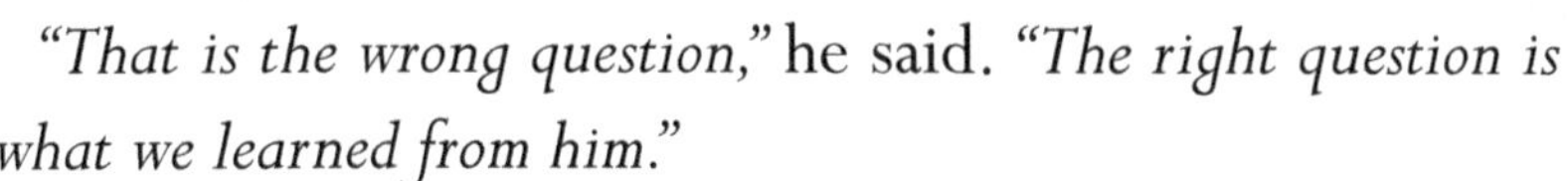

"That is the wrong question," he said. *"The right question is what we learned from him."*

Issac himself did not disappear entirely.

He lived simply now, far from centers of power. He walked through public spaces without guards. Some people recognized him. Most did not.

One afternoon, he sat on a bench overlooking a rebuilt district. Children played nearby. Their laughter echoed between clean buildings and open walkways.

A man approached hesitantly.

"You are him," the man said.

Issac looked up.

"Yes," he replied.

The man shifted his weight.

"I lost my brother during the wars," he said. *"I blamed you for a long time."*

Issac nodded.

"I understand."

"But my children are safe," the man continued. *"They eat. They learn. They are not afraid."*

Issac remained silent.

"I do not know if that makes you a hero or a monster," the man said.

Issac met his gaze.

"It makes me responsible," he said.

The man studied him for a moment, then extended his hand.

"I wanted to say that," he said. *"Nothing more."*

Issac shook his hand.

After the man left, Issac remained seated, watching the children run. Their arguments were small. Their concerns immediate. None of them carried the weight he once did.

That, he realized, was the measure of progress. The cost of Paradise was not whispered about anymore. It was discussed openly, in classrooms, councils, and private homes. The dead were named. The suffering acknowledged. The moral compromises examined without defensiveness.

In a televised discussion, a moderator posed the question plainly.

"Was it worth it?"

A panelist answered first.

"We live in a world without global war or hunger," she said. *"That matters."*

Another shook his head.

"We lost millions to get here," he said. *"That matters too."*

A third spoke quietly.

"Peace was not given to us," she said. *"It was built. And building anything costs something."*

That sentiment echoed across the world. It was a process and it required maintenance and accountability. It required people willing to resist comfort when comfort threatened justice and it required to be willing enough to

question authority even when authority claimed benev-
olence.

Issac now maintained a personal journal, written long after he relinquished control, there was no declaration of success. But there was only a reflection.

"I believed Paradise could be forced into existence," he wrote. *"I learned that it can only be sustained by choice. I gave the world tools. What it builds with them is no longer mine to decide."*

On a quiet evening, Issac stood at the edge of a community square as lights flickered on. People passed him without recognition. That anonymity felt earned.

A child ran past, chasing a ball.

"Sorry," the child said quickly.

Issac smiled.

"It is fine," he replied.

As the child rejoined the game, Issac looked around at a world still imperfect, still divided, still fragile. But alive and trying.

The question of whether Paradise was worth the cost

would never have a single answer. That uncertainty would remain, carried by generations who did not experience the world before change.

Perhaps that, too, was necessary. Because peace was never meant to be inherited without effort.

It was meant to be built. Again, and again.

And this time, together.